ELEVATED BY MY ENEMIES

THROUGH THE POWER OF GOD

Elevated by My Enemies Through the Power of God

Released – August 2019

Published by Final Step Publishing
P.O. Box 1447
Suffolk, VA 23439
www.finalsteppublishing.com

For Worldwide Distribution
Printed in USA.
ISBN: 978-1-7335842-1-0
Library of Congress Control Number2019931276

ELEVATED BY MY ENEMIES
THROUGH THE POWER OF GOD

Debra K. Jewell

Final
Step

Suffolk, VA

Preface

A
s I prepare to let God lead me in writing this book, I have to also keep in mind that the ultimate enemy, Satan, does not want it written. I have attempted to write this book for several years and never finished. Ultimately, I returned to complete the writings and, to my surprise, yet not to my surprise, the entire manuscript vanished from my computer. So, I am now more determined than ever to overcome the enemy of procrastination and complete this work the way God wants it to be done and in His time.

Looking back over my life, there are so many circumstances that I have had to overcome; people who have tried to cripple me; roads that I have traveled that tried to take me off course; and many thoughts and emotions that have raged through me that, at times, could have led me to call it quits and end it all. But faith in God, along with His favor, has kept me going and encouraged me to go on just a little further and a little longer. Deciding to become victorious and not a victim is easy to say, but not so easy to do when you have felt like a victim for most of your life. It truly takes God to pull you through and give you the strength to take each step towards a victorious life. It takes God to change your perception of self and to elevate you above your enemies.

In war, it is essential to know who your enemies are, what the collateral damage may be, and which strategies to use. As Christians, we know that the enemy (the devil) devises many traps and puts a target on our backs in an attempt to distract, deceive, and destroy. The Bible teaches us that he roams about like a roaring lion seeking whom he may devour. Knowing this, we must always be aware of him and his tricks. We also have another enemy called "ourselves." We, ourselves, are sometimes more dangerous than the evil one.

Moreover, life, circumstances, and people all have a way of interrupting our lives and clouding the reality of who we really are. As a result, and through the perception of mistaken identity, we become our own enemy by allowing the various curveballs of life to dim our view of who God designed us to be. Therefore, to overcome, we must adjust our focus and allow God to make the necessary changes in our lives. We cannot and should not attempt to do it alone as we are made to trust, rely upon, and have faith in God to rise above our enemies. God promised that, if we remain faithful to His will, His way, and trust Him with our lives, He would make our enemies our footstool (Hebrews 1:13). Nothing is too hard for God!

The first step in defeating the enemy is to recognize your opponent. Two scriptures to help on this are Proverbs 26:24-26, *"People may cover their hatred with pleasant words, but they're deceiving you. They pretend to be kind but don't believe them. Their hearts are full of many evils. While their hatred may be concealed by trickery their wrongdoing will be exposed in public"* and Deuteronomy 32:34-35, *"The Lord says 'Am I not storing up these things, sealing them away in my treasury? I will take revenge; I will pay them back. In due time their feet will slip. Their day of disaster will arrive, and their destiny will overtake them"* (NASB).

Most of life's battles are won or lost in the battlefield of the mind where there is a battle between flesh and spirit. In addition, to win the physical battle, we must learn to control the battle in the spirit. Proverbs 4:23 states, "Carefully guard your thoughts because they are the source of true life." 2 Corinthians 10:4 tells us that the weapons we fight with are not the weapons of the world. On the contrary, they have divine power to demolish strongholds. The word "stronghold" is derived from the Greek root ochuroma and means (N) castle or as a (V) to fortify. Paul's usage, in its literal translation, is a "prisoner locked by deception" (CEV).

We can win the mind game by studying God's Word, learning from our own experiences, and sharing in the experiences of others.

The LORD says to my Lord:
"Sit at My right hand until I make your enemies a footstool for your feet."
Psalms 110:1 NASB

TABLE OF CONTENTS

Introduction

I t is my hope and prayer that this book will be a blessing to all who open the pages and let the words become life to them. As God stirred up my spirit to look back over all of the things in my life that He has brought me through, I was able to see Genesis 50:20 at work, *"But as for you, you meant evil against me; but God meant it for good, God turned what the enemy meant for evil into my good."* It is tough to see things as they are when you are in the middle of a situation, but God has already written the story, and He works from the end to the beginning. As I go back and relive some challenging times in my life, I will only feel sad because they happened; but I can rejoice because God allowed me to prevail. As I share some of the situations that I've overcome, it is not my intent to put anyone on blast, or to air any dirty laundry, but, instead, to allow you to see how Jesus allowed me to be elevated by the enemies in my life.

All of us have a life story – good or bad. When I was in college, one of my professors, whose class I attended, required us to write our story from the perspective of there being "a party going on" when we were born. This was designed to help us understand that the world did not start when we were born because there were already things going on in the outside world. It was also to help us discover who we were in relation to our families, our issues, and our histories. Why was this important? It was so that we could discover and be delivered from the things (iniquities) that were haunting us and preventing us from being competent counselors to those we were going to serve. God also wants us to recognize the iniquities (sins and weights) that so easily beset us, so that those we serve are not the victims of our issues (enemies) and so that we can be effective Christians and witnesses for Christ.

God says to *"Sit at my right hand until I make your enemies your footstool,"* Psalms 110:1. This means that if we allow God to fight our battles, He will turn our tragedies into triumphs. In life, there will be many battles with various highs and lows. There will be times when you feel as though you'd rather crawl up in a cave and die. However, we must not die in the winters of our lives; instead, when things get

INTRODUCTION

tough, we, as believers, must turn to our living source, which is God in heaven. We cannot allow our enemies to take us out, nor can we lose heart and give up because we don't know the end. God has given us a gift of free will and, with it, we have the right to make choices –with or without God – and we should always choose to allow God to take us through the bad times to an expected end for this is His plan for our lives. So, as we travel this journey called life, God says choose whom you will serve, choose life or death, and accept blessings or curses. Will your enemies defeat you, or will you choose to let God make your enemies your footstool?

> The LORD says to my Lord:
> *"Sit at My right hand until I make your enemies a footstool for your feet."*
> Psalms 110:1 NASB

Chapter One

The Party

When I was born, a party had been going on for some ten to fifteen years before my birth. I was the first girl after five boys, and the party was in full swing. My father was the deejay, my mother was the party planner, and the rest of us were the guests. It was a big party as there were now six children and two adults in a small flat in the inner city of New Jersey. With five boys so close in age, I am sure that the party was often loud, rambunctious, and it was easily able to get out of hand. The deejay often playing the music of alcoholism would also be loud and riotous, to say the least. The party planner tried to hold it all together whenever the party seemed to get a little wild. I can't say for sure how loud the music was playing at the time or how chaotic it may have become; I can only speak to the status of it as I got older to appreciate all that was happening around me.

When I was two and a half, the party moved from New Jersey to a little town right outside of Richmond, VA. Being too young to understand the full impact of the "hows and whys" of the move, I can only imagine how it changed the atmosphere of another party held by my maternal grandfather and grandmother. Imagine taking six children from urban city life to a five-acre farm that was established as the family's home place. It may have seemed to be the perfect place for five lively boys to run, play, and burn off some energy, but the party planner saw it as a refuge, an escape if you will, and a place where the deejay's music could be minimized and kept somewhat under control. Shortly after arriving, however, things changed after my grandmother became ill and passed away. About a year later, with another baby on the way, my grandfather sold off his animals and moved into the city. This became a turning point in our lives. Without the protection of a bouncer, grandfather, and uncles, the music grew louder, the oldest boys became teenagers, and my mother seemed to be losing the fight to keep the party from getting out of control.

Alcoholism had a firm grasp, and we all danced to its tune. My father, without the restraints of the elders, became more violent and abusive. The deejay's music was getting louder and louder. As my brothers got older, they became a band of brothers who stuck together and protected my mom and younger siblings. By now, my younger sister was born, and we were a family of nine. The party was definitely out of control by this time. Our names had been changed; we were no longer called by our given names, but by the names given to us by the monster of abuse through the induction of alcohol. The swift erosion of the family was imminent; we quickly learned to take cover to protect ourselves, and we were always on guard, never knowing what the next moment would bring.

There were, however, some bright spots, and they would mostly come on Sundays. My mother would dress us up in our Sunday's best, and we went to the family church. My father would not go, of course; he was worshipping the bottle and most Sundays he would be "sleeping off" his Saturday. I, however, loved Sunday School and going to church. But the best part of all was seeing my Poppa. I can still see him now – standing like a stately gentleman in front of the church, waiting for us to arrive, with a pocket watch in one pocket and quarters in another. We would grab the quarters, give him a big hug and kiss, and run to the corner store to buy penny candy before Sunday school started. Sunday school was always fun as we learned who Jesus was and how He loved us. During the summer, we found refuge in Vacation Bible School, the annual homecoming services, and dinner on the grounds. People would come from near and far, and it would always make life a little better to see family and friends whom we hadn't seen since the last annual homecoming.

The church was a refuge for me, and it was a place where I could escape to get away from the raging craziness at home. It was especially comforting for me as I began to hear about Jesus and how He loved me and cared for me. This is where I learned the song, "Yes, Jesus Loves Me," and I would often sing it to shut out the deejay's music. This is also where I began to learn Bible verses and Bible stories of how Jesus would save me and keep me from harm. This is where I developed the foundation of my spiritual beliefs that would later protect me and deliver me from my enemies. God had already set the stage to give me a hunger and thirst for Him and to give me hope and a future. Of course, I didn't understand it then, but the Lord was putting things deep inside of me, even as a young child, that would be what I would need to survive and to rise above many adversities that would be designed to destroy or kill me. It was here that I heard the pastor say during a revival that Jesus could save me from hell. Therefore, at the age of eight, I accepted Jesus as my Lord and Savior and began my journey as a believer. I heard a message that night that I still remember today. My mother didn't think I understood my decision, but when the pastor questioned if I understood, I told him that I had accepted Jesus because He loves me and that He was going to save me from going to hell. Now, I may not have fully understood hell as a place where souls go when they have not accepted Jesus, but I did fully understand that I was in a living hell at home. It was the hope against hope that Jesus could save me from that hell!

I was an avid reader, and by the time I entered elementary school, I was reading on a fifth-grade level with full comprehension of what I read. Every day during recess, I was escorted to the fifth-grade class to show them how reading was done. I would read anything – encyclopedias, dictionaries, magazines, and newspapers – and I would read the Bible and then teach what I read to my youngest brother and my sister. I'd teach my dolls, the pets, and anyone who would listen. Although I read and understood, I also had a distorted view of "religion" and fundamental Christianity. This was because the deejay, through alcohol, would often distort the Word and use it to scare the living daylights out of those of us who now remained at home. He would rant in his drunkenness about God and how he was going to write a book called "The Thunder," because we were "destructive bastards," and "we weren't worth the power it took to blow us to hell." According to the deejay, whenever there was a thunderstorm, the thunder was a sign that God was going to strike us. Needless to say, I was afraid of storms for most of my life, as he would always wait until there was a thunderstorm to present us with this dissertation. Reading was my way of escaping and blocking out the words that were hurled my way, the rants hurled at anyone who stood in the line of fire, and the hell I lived in every day. However, reading would often introduce contradictions. These were not contradictions in content but contradictions in life itself. This was especially true when I read the Bible because I couldn't understand how God, and Jesus, who the Bible said loved me unconditionally, could allow me, allow us, to live in so much turmoil. I didn't fully understand faith at that time, I had childlike faith, but my understanding often superseded my religion.

With understanding came knowledge and wisdom beyond my years. I began to understand the signs of things going on at the party that should have been beyond my scope of knowledge. For instance, I knew if the deejay didn't come home at night, most likely, he was held up in the city jail for being drunk in public. If he stayed for a couple of days, he would always come meandering home with a bag of groceries that included a box of chocolate-covered cherries for my mother, and caramels for my sister and me. I understood that if he came home intoxicated, there would be hell to pay until he ran out of steam and fell into a drunken stupor and that someone would have to "clean him up" later that night. Usually, that job fell to the number four brother because he was the oldest sibling at home at this time. It was a messy and foul job that my mother refused to take part in, and yet, it had to be done.

I began to understand that my father spent more time with my baby sister than he did with me, and there were times when I knew that something was just not right with that picture. I began to understand that as much planning as my mother did to keep the peace in the home, she was unable to keep the party under control. I began to understand and know that what happened at home stayed at home, and that life outside of the household was quite different than inside behind closed doors. I realized that my mother soon would have to go outside of the home to work if we wanted to eat, and that I would become my sister's caretaker as the older siblings began to leave home. I understood and knew that my siblings were leaving, and the protection of my sister and I was leaving with them. I knew that as happy as I would be to see my older brothers come home to visit, I could be sure that their visits would probably end in violent fights and they would leave with the promise to never return. I understood that my mother was beginning to feel more and more helpless at home, and it left us younger ones more vulnerable to the vicious verbal, and often physical, attacks from my father.

The home around us was deteriorating fast – not just the family unit, but the physical home as well. We struggled to stay warm in winter and often had to cut our own firewood to heat the home. Usually, my father would pick up scrap wood or railroad ties to be burned in the woodstove, but because they were covered in tar, the room would become smoky and smelly and set the chimney on fire which was very scary! The kitchen had an old electric stove that would spit sparks from the outlet if there were a thunderstorm. Yes, on top of the raging storm inside and outside, there was fire coming from the plug of the stove. The bathroom became inoperable as the floor rotted and the septic tank eroded. My mother did her best to get things repaired by calling on my uncles, friends, and neighbors, but the music was now blaring out of control, and it appeared there would be no change or hope in sight.

My father rented a port-a-potty, supposedly until he finished repairing the bathroom, but that didn't happen! As I became a teen, now the oldest at home, it became my responsibility to keep things at home running while my mother was out working. This was included keeping my sister and myself out of the way of the raging beast. It was my responsibility to come home and light the kerosene heater so that the house would be warm for us and, in some cases, cut the firewood for the woodstove. It was also my responsibility to make sure we ate and did our homework. One day, not long after school had started for the next school year, my sister and I got off the school bus and raced each other up the hill to be the first to use the port-a-potty. As we both got to it at the same time, I flung open the door to push her aside. To our surprise and horror, there was the deejay sitting on the throne but slumped over and not responding to our calls. I raced into the house and called my mother, who was still at work to report what we found. She instructed us not to bother him and not to go back out to where he was. Later, when she came home tired from working, cleaning, and cooking for someone else, she checked on him and left him alone. My oldest brother had returned home from the Air Force, and when he came in that night, my mother instructed him to check on our father and to take a blanket to throw on him until he came out of his stupor this time. My brother went out and shortly rushed back in to tell my mom that she should call the ambulance as the deejay had slumped more and had a blue tongue. The next thing I remember was going to the hospital with the family to hear that my father had succumbed to liver failure because of drinking for so many years. Many emotions filled me that night – feelings of relief, despair, certainty, uncertainty, elation, disappointment, and fear. I wasn't sure how I was supposed to feel.

During the time of his funeral, I refused to shed a tear and was upset with my siblings for showing emotions that I couldn't understand. I felt that the party was now shut down. I thought that I could finally breathe a breath of relief for not having to live through the horrors of the deejay's music that had gotten way too loud, way too abusive, and way too long. I felt that the party planner had also taken a breath, with mixed emotions, and at times, she held her breath not knowing what was now in store.

At the time, I was fifteen years old and, though I didn't realize it then, I had become very angry. I was angry at my father for the things he did and the things he did not do, and angry at my mother because I felt that she didn't do enough to protect us from his abuse. Around this time, I also realized that I had been angry with my mother since I was approximately five years old and had refused to hold a conversation with her until after the funeral. I was angry that life was now uncertain, and that change was coming too fast. I was angry at learning that I would have to leave all of my friends that I had known most of my life and go to a different school. I was angry that our family was chosen to be the first to integrate the public schools we now attended. I was angry because I was of mixed ancestry and didn't feel as if I belonged to any race of people. Black people, yes, my friends, called me "White," and White people called me the "N" word. I became angry that people would stare at me all of the time to try to decide what race I was and then continue to stare until I stared back.

With all of this pent-up anger, I became rebellious and very distrusting of people. By this time, I was so angry with my mother that she couldn't tell me anything. I started drinking, hanging out for two or three days at a time, sleeping all day, and being out all night. I became a Black Panther; I became a revolutionist and activist. I became a Muslim, I became a Catholic, and I became a Universalist. Basically, I became anything out of the norm. Because of my mother's codependency, though my father was now deceased, I began to realize that even though changes had taken place, the party was still going on. It was as if the record had scratched and it was stuck on the same verse playing over and over and over.

Nothing seems right in the average fifteen-year old's mind, but because I was well versed, and above average intellectually, I began hanging with an older crowd and seeking things to make the music stop playing in my head. I ran wild, and I ran hard. There was no looking back for this kid. I was like a caged bird set free, spreading its wings and going too far too fast and not knowing or caring where it was going. I just knew that I was set free from the hell that I had witnessed for the past fifteen years. At least I *thought* I was free. Not knowing anything about iniquities, curses, or bloodlines, I continued on a path of destruction that would go well into adulthood. I couldn't understand myself because I didn't know myself. I couldn't heal because I didn't realize I was broken. I didn't know that because of MY bloodline, MY history, and MY predetermined participation in the party going on even before I was born, I would be haunted for years to come.

All of this was a part of who I became and the enemies in my life that I would have to fight to overcome. There would be many enemies and afflictions such as the enemies of low self-worth, low self-esteem, low confidence, self-destruction, poverty and lack, AND the enemy that roams about seeking whom he may devour. In the next few chapters, I will discuss how the enemies of my life were developed, designed, and designated to steal, kill, and destroy. Then finally, I will explain victory, triumph, and becoming an overcomer, by the blood of the lamb, and by this, my testimony (Revelations 12:11).

Chapter Two

Iniquities

niquities are defined as gross injustice or wickedness; a violation of right or duty; a wicked act; sin that is passed down through the bloodline (Dictionary.com). Etymologically, it is customary to explain iniquity as literally meaning crookedness or perverseness. It is evil regarded as that which is not straight or upright; it is a moral distortion. Iniquity is that thing that stirs up desires and passions that lead to transgressions. Transgressing is putting those iniquities into action that become the sins and weights that so easily beset us by going beyond the bounds and limits of God's Law. It is that habitual sinfulness and those things that get a grip on us that take the power of God to break. Examples include addictions, such as alcoholism, sexual immorality, drug abuse, abuse (physical, mental, emotional), lying, stealing, killing, anger, and curses. They are those ugly truths that are passed from generation to generation, and those character flaws that we will see. These are the things that as children, or even as adults, we may have heard said like this, "You're just like your mother, father, uncle, grandparent, etc." We all inherit these character flaws through our blood. When Adam sinned in the Garden of Eden, sin passed down to all men, and therefore, we are ALL born with the natural ability to sin. David said in Psalms 51:5 that he was born in sin and sharpened in iniquity.

Our lives are often shaped by the iniquities that have a long root in our family tree. Unfortunately, trying to eradicate the system of these iniquities can appear daunting. This is mainly because the source is not dealt with and treatment of any kind attempts to alleviate the symptoms, not the root. Many attempts may be made to address the symptoms but, just like trying to kill weeds in a garden, if the root is not pulled up, it will spring up repeatedly and may eventually take over. How many times have we known someone dealing with alcoholism or drug addiction, who has made many attempts to get, and remain, clean only to succumb to the lure of drugs or alcohol? That leaves the person or generation in a perpetual state of recovering without complete deliverance. We are all prone to some type of sin or iniquity. That's our sinful nature! Our parents were "iniquities" married to "iniquities" that commingled and perpetuated to the next generation. In Deuteronomy 5:9-10 God says, *"You shall not worship them or serve them; for I, the Lord your God, am a jealous God, visiting the iniquity of the fathers on the children, and on the third and the fourth **generations** of those who hate Me, but showing loving kindness to thousands, to those who love Me and keep My commandments."*

The iniquities that formed my character were my dad's alcoholism and my mom's codependency. This developed a tendency in me to be drawn to men that had character flaws similar to my father, who were abusive, mean spirited, and drank too much. I inherited the need for love, and the acceptance of bad behavior, from my mother, who once told me, it was better to have a bad marriage, than not to have a marriage at all. I took my place at the party and became what I considered normal. As much as I hated the days of the loud party of alcoholism, I began to drink, later played around with recreational drugs, and sought the affection of men.

Along with all of this was a spirit of low self-worth. Having been told for as long as I could remember by my father that I wasn't worth the power to send me to hell, it destroyed any confidence that I had to believe in myself. Now I may not have known at first, what that meant, but if you tell a child something long enough, they will believe it sooner or later. Although I'd been told most of my life how attractive I was, how smart I was, and how "pretty" my hair was, none of it could erase those recordings of the rages of alcohol telling me I wasn't worth much. I had no confidence in others, or myself, and it became a driving force in how I reacted to people and situations. My mother didn't make things much better as I seemed to be a thorn in her side.

Due to my ability to comprehend things through reading, I was often questioning things that seemed contradictory to something I learned. I would get excited about learning new information, and I had no one with whom I could share. My mother was busy just trying to cope with a large family, a husband that was not meeting the needs and demands of the family, and maybe even questioning her own choices she'd made. With all of this weight on her shoulders, she found it difficult to be encouraging and supportive. I should have been daddy's little girl being the first girl after five boys; however, I was anything but that, and as I grew older, I began to realize that it probably was a good thing I wasn't.

Until you discover that you are operating out of the iniquities of your bloodline, you will continue to repeat behaviors that are not conducive to you being successful in every area of your life. Very few, if any, have found complete success. They may be successful in one area but lacking in another. You may have all of the money that you desire and be able to meet your physical needs, but your emotional needs may be a complete shipwreck. You may have your emotional state healed but be living in poverty. Alternatively, you may have the money and the marriage, but cancer, that runs in the family, has raised its ugly head. Truth be told, we will never have it all together because we are flawed creations. However, if we can learn to yield our lives to the One who can provide, heal, protect, and break curses, we will live contented lives.

Have you ever thought that you had arrived and then suddenly, something came to pull the rug from under you? I have, and if it hasn't happened, as the old folks used to say, keep living. About twenty years ago, I thought I had arrived in my little world. I had a fantastic job where I traveled the country presenting a new program and I had just bought a house and a car. Life was good! One day, after moving into my house and unpacking all day, I was taking a box up into the attic and just as I got to the middle of the stairs the spring moved, I lost my balance, and as I turned to jump, I realized that I was too far up to safely jump. Life changed suddenly! I severely broke my leg to the point that, though the doctor never said it, the therapist questioned if I would be able to walk again. This became a time of learning to trust God in every situation! I had to trust Him as I lost my job, finances, and often came to the brink of giving up not knowing what I had to face each day. I bought a very expensive vacuum cleaner from someone who came by to clean my house and help me out. I don't even remember buying it as I was on powerful pain medications at that time. A breaking point came when I had paid out all of my bills and the bank called to say that the vacuum company had put a lien on my checking account and none of the bills, I had sent checks for, would clear. I was livid and did not know what to do. I had no more funds, had not received any notice of the lien, and had to get up out of my sickbed to go to court to have it reversed. My house, my lights, and my water were all threatened because of that act. In the meantime, I received a notice from the electric company for a $5000.00 electric bill! Yes, I said five thousand dollars! It turned out to be an error; however, it was at a time when I was already at a breaking point, and it was the last straw! I was pre-disposed to be depressed, and depression set in big time. I did not know how to handle what I was going through. I was already dealing with a life-changing incident of not walking and being active as I was usually, and now my finances were nearing non-existent.

Looking back now, I see that it was all a setup for God to teach me to trust Him. I stumbled through, I crawled through, I fell through, I prayed through, and I cried through, but I made it through! God showed me that even though I was going through a dark time in my life, He was still there to take me through. He was a light shining through the darkness. He promised never to leave me or forsake me, and He didn't. He sent people to aid in helping me through to make sure I did not lose my car, my house, or my mind.

I was not taught how to handle difficult times, I was not taught how to manage money, and I was not taught how to trust God by my natural parents. They were too busy carrying out their roles during the "party." As invited or uninvited guests, we were left to stumble through life and get it the best way we could. Some of us got it financially but suffered emotionally. Others got it financially but didn't put the principles of God to it and lost it. Others turned to drugs and alcohol, sex, and other addictive behaviors. I struggled emotionally and financially. Not having much as a child, wanting and liking nice things, I never had enough and always spent what little I had. I was addicted to shopping to make me feel better emotionally.

The iniquities that we all have will take over if we let them! We must recognize those things in our lives that are constant enemies such as those addictions, hindrances, and weights that hold us back from being free to live the lives God designed and predestined for us. We often go through life excusing, adjusting to, and living with those very things designed to defeat us when the Bible states that we are overcomers by the blood of the lamb and the word of our testimonies. Whom the Son sets free is free indeed; but, even when we have an opportunity to be free, we often give in to the pull of the enemy and the temptations that cause us to fall back into the very things from which we have been set free.

We become familiar with our enemies and even fall in love with them. In psychology, this is called Stockholm Syndrome, and it happens when a captive begins to identify with his captor. We become comfortable with our enemies, identify with them, and accept their behavior, so when the doors are opened to freedom, we often choose to stay where we are. There is an idiom that states, "Familiarity breeds contempt." This means, the better we know people (things, situations), the more likely we are to find fault with them.[1] However, even when finding fault with them or even not liking them, we sometimes will stay stuck in a situation because we do not know how to get out. Many do not understand domestic abuse and will often question why someone would stay in a situation where they are being abused physically, mentally, and emotionally. Several

---

[1] The New Dictionary of Cultural Literacy

reasons include familiarity in the situation and fear of the unknown, identifying with the captor(s), and feeling that it is safer inside of that situation than out. I know some of you still don't understand, but unless you have been in that situation, don't judge. We are all held by something or someone that others would not understand. It might be a thought, an emotion like bitterness or anger, or it might be unforgiveness or the hurt of being abandoned by someone. Regardless of what it is, all of these and many more can be a source of captivity that becomes an iniquity in our lives.

Enemies come in many forms. Some are injected by life, some by people, some are self-injected, and, some even come from the ultimate enemy, the devil! Enemies are designed to steal, kill, and destroy! Sound familiar? They are designed to take us off track and to distract us from accomplishing that which God has intended for us to be and the work we are to do. When Adam fell, it separated him/us from a spiritual connection with God. The enemy, the devil, showed up in the garden and infiltrated the thought life and belief system that changed the original designs of our minds. Our thought life became skewed and began to control us rather than being controlled by the Spirit. The Bible states in Proverbs 23:7, *"For as he thinks in his heart, so is he"* (AMP). As we grew farther and farther away from the Spirit of God, we, in our own minds, began to worship ourselves, think without consulting God, and iniquities and sins developed in our bloodlines. These iniquities and sins will travel down to the third and fourth generations. Until we change the way we see ourselves and understand that the mind is a battlefield where sin starts with our thoughts, we are bound to continue to perpetuate the iniquities and sins of our ancestors. I don't know about you, but I have decided that it has to stop somewhere, and it might as well begin with me. I don't want to see my children, grandchildren, and great-grandchildren continue to struggle with the iniquities and enemies that have plagued my family for generations. It's time to set the captives free and let it begin with me!

Chapter Three

Identifying the Enemy Within

Many times, in life, some things will come against us. Many are out of our control; however, there comes a time that, even if we were victims of someone else's evils, we have to stop being the victim and become the victor. It is easy to place the blame on others as this puts the responsibility of our hurts and our reactions on the perpetrators. Often those perpetrators have gone on with their lives in whatever capacity, yet the victim is continuing to carry the pains well into life, and their life is showing it. This is not to downplay any circumstance that may have happened beyond our control; this is to show how these circumstances can control how we act, think, and operate in life. If we do not get a handle on things, we will continue to go around in circles and continue to live defeated in many areas of our lives. Jesus said that He came to give us life and life more abundantly. Aren't you ready to live an abundant, victorious life?

For many years there were areas in my life that, no matter how hard I tried, I just could not get right. There still are some areas. We are all a work in progress. However, I became sick and tired of being sick and tired of going through the same wilderness year after year. I can imagine how the Israelites must have felt continuing to go around the same mountain for forty years. It appeared that things happened in my life that was out of control, and I often wondered if I was cursed. I could not figure it out; I could not shake it off no matter how hard I tried. With every New Year, I would make a resolution to "get it right this year." I would hear a pastor say at Watch Night Service how this was going to be "my" year and I wanted to believe it; maybe, this time it would come true. Well, year after year came and went and crazy things kept happening to me, things that seemed out of my control! The beginning of the turnaround came years later when I began to search inward to determine if I had anything to do with what was going on in my life. The first step was to recognize that I did not have a relationship with the Father, Son, and Holy Ghost. I was saved at eight years old, and I diligently went to church even when others in my family did not go.

However, I began to realize that I was just a churchgoer! I knew about God and Jesus, I said I loved them, and yet I only knew about them; I didn't really know them. Therefore, I began to really study the Word, developed a prayer life, and learned to apply the goodness of the Word to my life. That took some time, and though layers of my defenses were being peeled off, those layers ran deep. Chapter One is only part of the story. After studying the Word and learning to apply it to my life, I developed a greater appreciation of who the Father and Son were, but the relationship with the Holy Spirit didn't come until recently. I knew about the Holy Spirit, I respected the person of the Holy Spirit, I had seen the Holy Spirit at work, but I didn't really know the power of the Holy Spirit in me until now.

Once I developed a relationship with God, and his Son, I began to look retrospectively into my inner self. I began to ask God to allow me to see myself as He saw me. I asked Him to show me the areas that I needed to change to be all that He had designed me to be. Be careful asking for this because, when God begins to show the true self, it is not a pretty sight! God is so wise and merciful that He reveals us to ourselves in increments because, if He did it all at once, we would not be able to handle the stench. It is an ugly sight, and it can be overwhelming. So, He began to show me a small area at a time. I began to see that I was very immature, I was spoiled, and wanted to continue to be spoiled, and that I was stuck emotionally as a child. I began to hear conversations I was having as if I were an ear outside of myself. My voice was very tiny and squeaky, and I talked like a child. It got to a point where it irritated me to the point that I began to change. I was always very quiet as a child, not comfortable talking to people, and I carried that over into adulthood until I decided to make changes that would change my voice, language, and my attitude. I began to build confidence by joining in conversations that were more mature and learned how to project my voice. I went back to school to obtain my degree and stepped out on my own to rebuild my life and to dispel the lies of the enemies within. Gradually, I began to work on the areas that God would reveal to me. Some areas were harder than others and took more time. Some iniquities had solid roots that were not easily plucked out. Other areas were a matter of thinking, acting, and believing differently and seeing myself as God sees me.

As I've mentioned before, God bestowed above-average intelligence upon me as a child. By the time I was four years old, I was reading and comprehending on a third-grade level. Because I was able to comprehend, I would also ask questions to further my understanding and to get feedback that I was on the right track. I would often turn to my mother for reinforcement and support; however, most times, she was too occupied with the cares of life to be able to provide the help I needed. My brothers were often gone or out playing around. By five years old, I began to understand conversations and my environment. I started to see things that, at five, I shouldn't have seen, hear things I shouldn't have heard, and ask questions I shouldn't have asked. This is where the blank spots in my childhood begin. One day, while seated at the kitchen table, where I read most of the time, I asked my mother a question about the relationship between my father and my baby sister. I wanted to know why he spent so much time with her, why he always sat her on his lap to read to her, and why was I not allowed to go into the room. The answer was a slap that knocked me out of the chair and a warning to never ask those questions again. From that point on, I had very little words to say to my mother for a very long time, years, and nothing to say to adults unless forced. My world began to crumble at five years old. The party had turned ugly!

When I entered school, my reading was so advanced that my primary teacher would call me from recess each day to go read to the fifth-grade class to show them how reading "is done!" At school, I found reinforcement; however, by this time, I was so withdrawn, especially around adults, that it hindered my progress. In third grade, two other students and I were at the top of our class and were considered for promotion. or "being skipped" as we called it. All I remember is that each of us had to have our parents come and talk with the teacher and principal, and a decision was made about us being promoted or not. My mother came, my father did not, and after the conferences, all I know is that my two friends were promoted, and I was not. I was devastated and dejected. I became angrier with my mother because she would not explain to me the reason why I was not promoted, and I began to lose confidence in myself. Still trying to win the approval of my mother, I had shut my father out by this time. I would go to her with information that I had learned to only be rebuffed with the phrase "Oh, you think you're so smart!" That is a phrase that would come to haunt me for many years. Anger was now piling on top of anger. There was a mixed bag of emotions going on inside of this nine-year-old. I was so angry inside; I was feeling unloved and even unwanted by my parents.

By this time, self-destructive behaviors were setting in, I was learning that I could not trust the love of my father because he had disappointed me, and our family, too many times, and I felt that my mother wasn't protecting us. I would have thoughts of running away and never coming back. There were times I would scratch up my arms and face to try to remove the pain. Almost daily after school, I would dread going home not knowing what music was playing. I learned low self-worth, my self-esteem bottomed out, and I seethed at the compliments on my hair, my looks, or my intellect. To add insult to injury, our family was one of the first to integrate the public schools in our county. I was split from the few dear friends I had because of the school change, and I learned about segregation on a completely new level. I no longer belonged to any group of people. I was too light skinned to be included in being a "Negro" and too dark-skinned to be included elsewhere. My "colored" friends called me a White girl, and my eyes weren't the right color to be White, so I was called the "N" word by the Caucasians. Imagine not fitting in at home and not fitting in at school. God is so faithful because on a fall evening at a little church in the country, this little misfit found a loving God who took her into His family and called her His own.

As I began to wrap myself in God's love, even as a child, I began to feel God's presence around me, and it was the safest place to be. When I became afraid of the chaos around me, God allowed me to feel peace and to shut out the noise of my life. I used to tell my mother that God spoke to me often and that He told me that I was His special child.

However, I fell into the trap of low self-worth, this was learned behavior, and it took some time and work to come out of the fog to see and learn that I was fearfully and wonderfully made. After recognizing some of the patterns in my life that were contrary to who I really was, I began to do some soul-searching and searching God's Word. As I began to learn myself – learning my strengths and weakness, my likes and dislikes, my passions and my struggles –I started to work on these things systematically and with God's direction. Thankfully, I have changed many of those patterns in my life. I realized that I did not become that way overnight, and it would take some time to work through them. I had to have patience with myself, and with God, who was reshaping and re-molding the way I thought. The Bible says that as a man thinks in his heart, so is he (Proverbs 24:7) and I realized through the process that I didn't know much of my worth. I had to step away from all male/female relationships to focus on myself. As I went through during that time, I asked God to cover me, and He did.

It is crucial to identify your own enemies. I'm not only talking about people and demons, but also the enemies in your mind. Those are the enemies that have become your thought patterns, habits, and any other self-destructive behaviors. Often, situations and circumstances can dictate whom or what becomes our enemy. A key part of Proverbs

24:7 is that as a man thinks in his heart, so is he. Therefore, if life issues have broken your heart, you can begin to identify yourself by those issues. Proverbs 4:23 states that we are to *"Watch over your heart with all diligence, for from it flow the springs of life."* One translation says that from it flow the issues of life! If, as a child, you suffered rejection, as I did, you start to think of yourself as unworthy of any sincere love. Ultimately, heart issues become head issues, and the recordings in your head will begin to establish your thoughts and beliefs of who you think you are and who you will become. Many talents and dreams have died and gone to the grave because people did not believe in themselves to fulfill their true destiny. This occurs when the enemies of low self-worth, low self-esteem, fear, and doubt take up residence in your heart and thought life. Until you identify the enemy and change your heart and thoughts toward yourself, you will set up patterns and behaviors that can cause you to become stuck and stagnant in your growth and maturity.

To prosper in every area of your life, you must seek God for complete healing. Complete healing comes in different stages. It takes time, and it is a process that will be determined by how much you want to be healed entirely, and by the effort, you put in it. We will often grow in a particular area and leave other areas untouched. For instance, we may mature financially yet leave our emotions in a state of perpetual chaos, or we may grow emotionally and still have unforgiveness in our hearts. Only through God's love and by learning who He says we are, do we become healed in our mind, will, and emotions.

It's time to know who you really are in Christ. You were born into eternity, you are fearfully and wonderfully made, you are the head and not the tail, you are above and not beneath, you are the righteousness of God. My heart began to rejoice, and I kept putting God's Words in my mind thinking on them repeatedly to change the previous recordings that I believed about myself. Gradually, my heart began to heal, and I began to believe the things God said about me. As my heart healed, my thought patterns and behaviors started changing, and I started to mature in my emotions so that what I used to think about myself also adapted. 2 Corinthians 5:17 states, *"Therefore if anyone is in Christ, [a]he is a new creature; the old things passed away; behold, new things have come new"* (NASB). I was becoming a new creature.

Regardless of the battles that you must fight, and in spite of the voices that have been playing in your head, Romans 12:2 (NIV) states, *"Do not conform to the patterns of this world but be transformed by the renewing of your mind. Then you will be able to test and approve what God's will is—his good, pleasing, and perfect will."* If you want to be whole, let God transform your mind. Change your negative recordings to positive affirmations by thinking about who you are, and what God says about you! God created you, and you are fearfully (greatly) and wonderfully made. You are the head and not the tail! You've been adopted into a royal family, and all of the rights of the Kingdom are yours! Ask the Father to transform your mind and to set you on a course to liberate you and set you free! You can overcome those internal enemies that have been holding you back! You are victorious over your enemies.

Chapter Four

Recognizing the External Enemies

W e live in a world that seems to be full of obstacles, evil seems to abound at every turn, and people appear to be becoming more corrupt daily. Many things rise up against us and, on most occasions, life just doesn't seem fair. The rich are getting richer, often from the pockets of the poor, and the poor are getting poorer from the greed and deceptions of the rich. As a result, trying to survive has become a vicious cycle.

Afflictions come in many different forms, and if we give in and focus on them, we will become overwhelmed and defeated. Yet, the Word of God is given to help us handle every affliction. The Word is full of precepts, statutes, and laws of God. In Psalms 119:71, David states, *"It is good for me that I have been afflicted; that I may learn thy statutes"* (ASV). Job tells us in Job 36:15, *"But by means of their suffering, he rescues those who suffer. For he gets their attention through adversity"* (NLV).

When we are afflicted by circumstances of life, we should turn to God, and His Word for that's where we will find strength, joy, and peace. The Word is God's promise to help us move from faith to faith and from glory to glory. Afflictions are allowed so that we can grow in faith and develop trust in Him. If we never go through anything, then how would we measure our trust level? Scripture states that faith without works is dead. How can we work our faith if it's not put to the test? When we become God's children, as our Father, He provides us with everything we need, but there is a key to receiving those provisions. That key is the activation of our faith. He gives us His promises and if we don't believe them, put them in our hearts, and remember them during times of affliction, then they are just words in a book! It's like going to the gym, looking at the equipment, and never using it. We can read up and learn about each piece of equipment and what part of the body, it will enhance yet if we don't use it; it's just a nice piece of equipment. God's Word and faith are the same way. We can read and learn about how they can enhance our body, mind, and spirit, but if we don't put them into action, they're not going to be effective.

We must recognize that as children of God, we have an adversary, the devil that roams around seeking whom he may destroy. 1 Peter 5:8 says it this way, "Be sober, be watchful: your adversary the devil, as a roaring lion, walketh about, seeking whom he may devour" (ASV). He is always on the prowl, and every day, his imps receive their assignments to wage war against God's children. We must be vigilant and sober minded to recognize what that assignment may be and to resist the devil so that he has to flee. We cannot be overcome by afflictions, but we must use those times to draw nearer to God.

After we identify the enemy within, we also must recognize the external enemy. Do you always seem to attract the same kind of people, and tend to experience the same sort of drama in your life? Each time you develop a relationship, does it tend to turn out the same way? Each time you get over one drama is there another one that soon comes? Do you seem to suffer attack after attack in the same area? If this sounds familiar to you, then you may want to do a self-assessment and recognize what familiar spirits you are attracting. As stated before, the Bible says as a man thinks in his heart, so is he. We attract who we are! So, if you don't think much of yourself, guess what, you're going to attract those who don't either. Is everyone around you gossiping and complaining? Check yourself! Amos 3:3 states, *"Can two walk together unless they agree?"*

Later, as I began developing relationships, I began to take note of the people I surrounded myself with or who attached themselves to me. I would often get upset with people who were in my circle because they would be one of two kinds. They would either see me as a weakling and take advantage of me, or they would be very needy people who would take advantage of me. Because of things that were spoken to me, about me, and over me through my tumultuous childhood and young adult years, I believed some false truths. I believed out of my anger that I had to be mean and vindictive because that was learned behavior. It wasn't who I really was, however, so in an attempt to change that image, I went from being mean and vindictive to being meek and forgiving. The problem was that I went from one extreme to another, and I couldn't seem to find that balance until I began to look inward to see what I was attracting outwardly. What I found was that I didn't know who I was. I identified myself by who others said I was or who they thought I should be. Internally, I felt like someone was inside screaming to get out, but influences from the outside influenced the inside, and forces from the inside influenced the outside.

My mother and I had an extremely tumultuous and sometimes violent relationship during my teenage and young adult years. We would yell, scream, and fight with each other. I never could understand those times, and I often ran away in an attempt to emotionally and physically find solace elsewhere. My younger sister was seeking solace as well. As a teen, I began to hang in the streets, stay out days at a time drink and party as much as I could. I always knew I would hear it from my mother when I got home, so I just partied until I couldn't party anymore. I would escape by sleeping for a couple of days, and then before I could hear it again, I would be gone.

This all came at a time when the country was also at unrest. During the late sixties and seventies, rebellion was at an all-time high. My religious beliefs took a backseat to Black Power! This was a significant form of rebellion in our home. My mother was called to the school that I attended for a paper written on how the Black Power movement was beneficial. I was accused of plagiarism and was told to write another essay. I refused and stood my ground; however, my mother was very embarrassed. Mind you, this school's symbol was the rebel flag, and our family was one of the first families to be integrated into the White schools, so ultimately, I was once again trying to figure out where I fit in the family, life, and society. I took on the bad girl, Black Power image, which made me even more rebellious. I moved into the city with my family around the age of sixteen and went to a prominent high school in the area but, shortly after going there, integration came along with busing. I joined a movement that demanded better buses, better community centers, and I started seeking other religions. I sold bean pies as a Muslim, started catechism to become a Catholic, sat in a circle on the floor of the Unitarian Universalist Church, and returned back to the Baptist church. I was angry and searching for an identity.

As I stated before, you will attract who you are or who you perceive that you are. The energy or spirit that you put out will attract that back to you. My relationships reflected that. I attracted men that were all wrong for me--men who were older, rebellious, and married. Intellectually, I was much older than my age, though emotionally, I was still a child. Not until later, when I began to recognize destructive patterns, did I realize that because of my emotional immaturity and my intellectual maturity that I was searching for my father through my relationships with men. My natural father and I were never close as he vehemently denied that I was a part of him. By the time I was born, the deejay was playing a different tune. Five boys had preceded me, and alcoholism was the tune we were all singing. So, in his mind, filled with the destruction of alcohol, I represented his disappointment of having a daughter early on, not fulfilling his dreams, and his anger with the world. He had become verbally and sometimes physically abusive towards my mother, and eventually, I became the object of that frustration. Several of my uncles confronted him about being physical, but he learned that words could be just as powerful and hurtful. My sister was born a couple of years after me, and, unfortunately, she became the apple of his eye. It was unfortunate because he did things to her that no father should do to, or with, his daughter.

As I grew older and began to recognize the people and situations that I was drawn to, I began to question what was causing so much confusion and dysfunction in my life. Why was I experiencing the same things over and over? Why did it seem like I was going from mess to mess and from one situation to another? Why was I failing at so many things? What caused me to stay in a long term, thirteen-year, relationship I had no business being in, and why didn't I break the chains to get out? That's a story for another time. Nevertheless, I began to question my relationships with my mother, with other family members, with men, and even with myself. What did I need to do to change patterns of dysfunction?

The first thing I did was to recognize the patterns. I began to take a long hard look at how I perceived myself. I listened to the recordings in my head – those messages that drove me and the energy that I exuded from deep within. I began to pay attention to my speech, my behaviors, my dress, and my appearance. I began to change the messages I was receiving about myself and the messages I was sending out. After finding out that someone very close to me was dying from cancer, I sought out counseling to deal with her pending death. Although I went to learn how to deal with the loss, I ultimately used it as a tool to help change the negative messages I had heard all of my life and to put another record on to change the message. You see, I now had a party of my own going on, and I had stepped into the role of the party planner. I had to learn to love myself and not be defined by others. I also had to change some patterns that were sending the wrong messages and attracting the opposite of what I desired. I had to relearn years of thinking, uproot years of negative messages, and change patterns. It was not easy as these things had become who I was, and I had become them. I began to recognize, re-record, and reconstruct my very being.

Though I was a churchgoer, as mentioned before, I did not have a real relationship with Jesus. I was baptized and knew who Jesus was, but I did not have an intimate relationship with Him. I changed my attitude, I changed my location, and I was connected to a Bible-teaching church. I began to draw closer to God the Father, Jesus the Son, and Holy Spirit. As I began to delve into the Word of God and apply the Word to my life and situations, I slowly began to change, inside and out, and my perceptions changed. How I viewed my surroundings took on new pictures in my mind, which slowly began to change my heart. This all worked together to erase the negative messages that had been ingrained in the very depths of my soul and, over time, they were replaced with positive messages. The closer I got to God, and the more I developed an intimate relationship with Jesus, the more the Holy Spirit began to comfort me, guide me, and lead me to a place of healing. This was not an easy process, but it was a necessary process that I had to go through to recognize the external enemies that I was attracting from within myself. It was necessary so that God could take me from one state to another and reset the course of my life.

Chapter Five

Beginning the Healing Process

The beginning of any type of healing that promotes change is the recognition of what the problems are that are keeping you bound. For me, as stated in the previous chapters, there were many. My soul (mind, will, intellect, and emotions) was damaged beyond recognition due to the many circumstances of my life. Who I had become, a hurting, angry, and mean-spirited person, was not who I felt I really was. Deep inside was the real me feeling trapped, scared, alone, and screaming to get out. The more I tried to become different, the more I seemed to become tangled in who I was not. Being out of place on the inside developed character flaws that oozed to the outside. My low self-esteem and low self-worth were being reinforced by people, circumstances, and my own decisions. I kept doing the same things, making the same mistakes, and developing relationships with people who echoed the recordings being played in my subconscious. I became a people pleaser, yet I seethed inside because I wanted to be my own person. I wanted to do the things I wanted to do and make my own decisions. Instead, I was still fighting the battles of the inner and outer self.

Finally, after losing my best friend, who was the only support system I had at the time, I initially went into therapy to deal with her death, but it became a turning point in my life. After receiving grief support, I began to work on other issues of my life. I had come to the point where I was tired of failure, or feeling like a failure. I wanted to stop the recordings of self-doubt, no self-worth, and very low self-esteem. I now had two children whom I loved more than life, but I was beginning to realize that every mistake I made would affect them as well. I wanted out of the life I was living, but I didn't know how to change. Counseling helped me to walk through the layers of my life to begin to understand the hows and whys of certain behaviors. It was not easy to even begin the process of healing and change as it had taken years to develop and would take years to change the negative of thoughts and behaviors. All of the internal and external enemies would have to be put to flight, and they weren't going quickly. However, the change had begun, and it had to start with me.

As I began the process of self-assessment, I turned to prayer and supplication and asked God to give me the strength to go through the process and make the necessary changes. The first thing God began to show me was how I talked and interacted with others. As I heard myself, I began to hear the voice of a little child that was very immature and non-commanding. No one took me seriously or believed in me because I didn't believe in myself. I talked like a child, I looked like a child, and I made very immature decisions, like a child! My emotions were a mess, my thought processes were a mess, I was a mess. Still, like a child, I didn't know how to get out of the mess, so I continued to make bad decisions. Even as I looked at myself in the mirror, I didn't know the steps to change. I didn't like what I saw but that only compounded how I felt. I felt like Alice falling down the rabbit hole! I began to cry and cry out to God, and when I would go to church, tears would come streaming down, and I didn't know why.

I slowly began to change, almost without notice but, as I began to look at the outside differently, the inside began to change. That may sound a bit strange, maybe even the opposite of the norm, but I've never been a normal person. I remember walking down the street one day to get lunch, and I passed a storefront building and caught my reflection in the window. I was astonished at what I saw. It was as if seeing myself for the first time in natural light. I began to cry, and then I got angry at myself. The person that I saw was not the person that I perceived myself to be. I did not look attractive, I did not look like an adult, and I looked like I didn't care about myself at all. I asked myself what was really going on? How did I get this far out of character? I went right away and made a hair appointment, started tossing out clothes that were way out of style, and began to talk to myself in the mirror. Like David, after the battle of AI, I began to encourage myself. I was scheduled for major surgery, and I was determined that life after surgery would be different than before. I had to change my mindset, and I was decided to start immediately. The process was long and painful, but I had already begun the process, and it began with the way I saw myself, *"As a man thinketh..."* I hadn't thought much of myself, and my inner and outer man reflected my thoughts.

After surgery, I moved out of the area and started on a new journey. My new life had begun. I enrolled in college, which was something I had wanted to do for a long time. God opened the door to expedite housing after I was told it was a year-long waiting list. My family and I were now on the road to recovery; we were going on a transformation journey. I was not alone in this, and we all had to recover from my issues. My daughter was in her early teens, and my son was an adolescent at the time, so they had experienced a lot of the things I had been through. As I recovered from physical surgery, God had begun the operation on my mental and emotional self. I found a church in my neighborhood, and it was there that I sought strength for my spiritual needs. It was the beginning of a transformation that would take me on an amazing ride. God knew just what I needed to begin the process and to see it out. Jeremiah 29:11 says, *"For I know the plans I have for you," declares the Lord, "plans to prosper you and not to harm you, plans to give you hope and a future"* (NIV).

This scripture has come to life for me. I didn't see it at first; I didn't even know this at first. I learned this scripture during one of the series when my Pastor at the time, encouraged us to memorize God's promises for our lives. Often through the years, as I learned more about my relationship with the Father and the Son, I began to understand that God did have a plan for me – His plan, not mine! This was hard to understand or believe in the beginning because even though I had been saved as a child and attended church often, I knew *about* God but did not *know* God. I went to church, like so many do, and heard a good word, but I came out and tried to make things fit into my plan. It just didn't work! My plans were totally opposite to God's plans. My plans led to more death and destruction, while God's plans were trying to lead me to a future and a hope. God's tender mercies, His loving kindness, and His grace have led me on a triumphant journey. It wasn't easy, it wasn't a smooth path, but it was a new beginning.

Chapter Six

Rebuilding the Trust Factor

rust is a powerful thing! It will make or break a relationship. All relationships are built on a measure of trust. That measure is either developed and strengthened or broken and destroyed. When broken, it takes work and effort on all parties for that trust to be rebuilt. Sometimes it can be restored, and other times, no matter what happens, trust is permanently gone. Learning to trust can be the motivation to continue and further a relationship, or distrust can be so overwhelming that it can distort and skew the perception of what trust really looks like. Many times, our confidence in those who were supposed to help us to believe in them, or believe in ourselves, has been shattered. Whether through repeated disappointments, or other circumstances, trust was replaced with fear, shame, and doubt. This fear was of those who manipulated the trust factor and did or said harmful things that had a negative impact. This, in turn, led to shame and the belief that we cannot trust anyone, not even ourselves, along with doubt that anyone or anything can ever be trusted again. Trust will determine your belief system!

Breaking promises to a child will leave that child suspicious and doubting if anyone can keep their word. They are often pessimistic about the outcomes of their dreams and life in general. That cynical way of looking at things will most likely result in them living a defeated life. They will always see the glass half empty. It can also lead that person to doubt if God is real or that He will fulfill His promises for them. This type of attitude will often lead people to become negative about everything to the point of talking themselves right out of a blessing. Many times, they are very gifted and talented people. They are people God gave gifts to for the advancement of the Kingdom; however, they don't believe (trust) that God chose someone like them to use their gifts. Quite often they will hide behind a mask of false humility and try to excuse themselves from what God has called them to do by appearing to be unworthy, unqualified, and un-equipped to carry out an assignment. What they are really saying is that they are afraid to trust God, trust themselves, or trust you to believe in them to do the job. Do you know any of those people? I was one!

As I've stated earlier in the book, I grew up in a family that dealt with alcoholism. Trust left me at an early age. My father made promises that he never kept – promises that he would stop drinking, usually made on those rare occasions when he was sober, promises that we would take trips somewhere, promises that he would be home to bring food, but he would usually end up in jail, so food would come three days later. He made promises that he was going to restore the bathroom so it could be usable again, but he died in a port-o-potty that was rented for a job he promised to complete. In addition, my mother made promises too – promises that if we stayed out of his way and stayed quiet, there would be peace in the house, it didn't matter, promises that if we didn't listen to the mean and depraved things he said to us and about us they wouldn't define us, they did, and promises that if we kept quiet about what happened inside the home, it would magically disappear, it didn't. So, each day when we left the house, we believed that if we didn't tell what went on the night before, that when we returned, things would be different, but they weren't. Because of these many broken promises, we soon learned that we didn't know what to expect. These promises, spoken and implied, developed the expectancy that people, places, and things had no certainty to them. From this, mistrust was born. It took on the form of hurts, wounds, and scars that had developed over the years and took years to repair.

If hurts, wounds, and scars are not dealt with, they will soon develop into much more complex problems that can permanently affect one's life. When bitterness takes root, it becomes so entangled in our lives that it can utterly destroy us as well as those around us. When wounds suffered in childhood become intricately woven into our being and develop patterns in our lives, they become scars that will continue to affect us for the rest of our lives – or at least until we evaluate the quality of our life and establish what's working and what's not working in our lives. Once we do this, it's then time to start working on changing the recordings in our psyche that have set up destructive patterns and dominated our actions and behaviors for many years. We must believe that God is working things out for our good and, though we may have been wounded and scarred, He can do exceedingly, abundantly, above anything we can think or imagine.

In life, circumstances, events, and people will hurt you! It's a given that things happen, but how we handle them determines if they will take root and become deep wounds that scar us for life. If we let God help and heal us, we can move on in life and become whole. God is our only reliable source of healing. However, we must have the willingness to accept God's help and to take the necessary steps for change. You can read all of the self-help books ever written, and you can watch every show on T.V., but until you work the Word and establish your place in God, you will always live a defeated life. You've got to develop your faith to believe that you can and will be elevated above your hurts, wounds, and scars. Don't give yourself a pass to stay in your situation. Don't become comfortable while being crippled. Put your measure of faith to work and watch it grow. I've been in some low, dark places but, through God's Word giving me the strength to pull myself up and out of those places, I was able to come out. God took my struggles and made them a stepping stool to elevate me above everything I've been through.

Chapter Seven

Forgiveness and Restoration: Doing God's Will

U nforgiveness is a stronghold! Like an octopus, its many arms spread out in multiple ways and entangle our mind, body, and spirit. Unforgiveness can become debilitating and prevent us from reaching our full potential. It can also keep us from forming long-lasting and stable relationships and is known to cause many major diseases. When we carry unforgiveness around, it is like a backpack full of hidden treasures that we are afraid to put down and release. When this happens, we become afraid of trusting others and sharing the load. We walk around with the weight of it until we are all bent over like the woman in Luke 13:10-13 who had been crippled and bent over for eighteen years. Unforgiveness is toxic and will infect not only you but all those around you. Unforgiveness must be dealt with for full healing to take place.

For many years I could not understand why things were happening in my life to prevent me from progressing past a certain level. It seemed as if I would take one step forward and then ten steps back. I didn't realize that my thoughts, self-consciousness, and attitude toward certain circumstances, and people were controlling me and, therefore, my destiny. I've faced many circumstances that have caused a bitter root to develop. Ultimately, they became so much a part of me that I became familiar and comfortable with saying, "that's just who I am."

These circumstances included: growing up in a volatile home with a raging alcoholic, feeling unprotected from this monster by my mom, having a dysfunctional relationship with her, getting involved in inappropriate relationships, having miscarriages and a stillborn child, being sick unto near death on several occasions, and experiencing numerous other trials designed to take me out. There were many things designated to become enemies to kill my will, steal my destiny, and destroy my purpose. But God! In all of

His infinite wisdom, He kept me in the palm of His hand and protected me from being utterly destroyed. But I had to do my work!

I had to recognize the iniquities that came from my bloodline and begin to pray and denounce them in my life. I had to do self-assessments often, and with God's help, change the things that He showed me. I had to identify the external enemies as well as those within and slay them so that the healing process could begin.

One of the most important steps that I had to take was learning to forgive. Real forgiveness! Sometimes, we often say that we have forgiven something or someone, yet, when the subject of that thing comes up, and we soon realize it's still a sore spot! It doesn't matter if it's God, man, or circumstance that we're angry and bitter at, if it remains a sore spot, I would venture to say that it is not forgiven. Forgiveness does not mean that you brush away the matter, it means that you find peace in your heart towards the matter. Forgiveness must take place to heal and to grow. It is God's will that we prosper and be in good health, even as our soul prospers, 3 John 1:2, and being that our soul is made up of our mind, will, emotions, and intellect, this indicates that God wants us to be completely whole in every area. God commands us to forgive! There are many scriptures on forgiveness and why we should forgive such as Mark 11:25, Matthew 6:15 and 16:2, 2

Corinthians 2:10, Luke 11:4, and Matthew 6:12. In fact, a running theme throughout the Bible is forgiveness. Because of our sinful nature, we should ask God to forgive us. That being said, His Word says over and over that to be forgiven, we must first forgive. Unforgiveness is so destructive that it breaks families apart, destroys long term relationships and the formation of new ones, and it also destroys the body and soul. It will dim your spirit as it becomes a dark cloud that stemming from a bitter root of anger and possibly also resentment towards a person or thing.

I had to learn to forgive myself, my parents, and the circumstances that had become dark spots in my life. It took a lifetime for these things to become strongholds, so it wasn't easy to go back and remember some things that were hidden yet profoundly impacting my life. Some of these things were harder to address and to forgive, but it had to be done. Other things had to be sorted through to determine if they were or should even be impacting me at all, but the bottom line is, I had to sort through the cobwebs to see if they were essential to keep or throw away. It's like sorting through an old storage closet. As you make your way through the "stuff," you begin to sort through the things that are important to you and hold fond memories. There are other things you question keeping at all. Unforgiveness is the same way. Sometimes you have to go back and weigh the value of that thing and determine why it was such a source of pain. Surprisingly, there will be times when you find out that what you were holding on to really wasn't worth the weight, so it wasn't worth holding at all. Other things are much more challenging to let go of and need more time to work through. That's where God's help comes in. Those things that don't hold much weight can be eliminated in your own strength, but those that carry much weight can only be removed or circumcised out of our heart by God's love and His power.

Forgiveness is not so much for the other person but mainly for our own well-being. One of the major cancer treatment programs has forgiveness as one of their treatment modules. It recognizes how the bitter root of unforgiveness can cause cancer and prevent healing. God, who is the master crafter and designer of our spirit, soul, and body, also understand how forgiveness can bring us into a right relationship with Him and with our fellow man. It is God's will that we have peace and life abundantly. Though the enemy seeks to steal, kill, and destroy, Jesus came to give us abundant life (John 10:10), so that we can live life to the fullest with nothing broken and nothing missing.

Though the enemy came to rob me of peace, murder my purpose, and destroy God's plan, these attempts have only made me stronger and created a warrior in me. I stand today full of the life that God promised. Yes, I had to forgive some hard situations that were imposed on me. Yes, I had to forgive my father for abandoning me and rejecting me. But I've found a Father who loves me unconditionally and promised to never leave me or forsake me. I've forgiven my mother who, in my child's eye, didn't protect us from the beast, and I've come to realize that she did the best she could under the circumstances. I've forgiven myself for allowing certain people, places, and things to identify me and for following their lead – I have learned who I am in Christ. I've had to repent and even asked God to forgive me for the times that I became angry at Him for allowing things to happen in my life.

We are commanded to forgive others so that we are forgiven. Forgiving my father was the hardest thing to do. I didn't want to forgive him! Several of my siblings went to his grave and talked to him. They even cried and were cleansed that way as they sought to forgive him and his impact on their lives. I never wanted to go to his grave, and I never felt the need to go back to that place, but there was a place that I needed to go to…my heart!

One night while in communion with my Heavenly Father, God began to minister to my heart. I had recently heard a message that said that the relationship I had with my earthly father would reflect the relationship I had with my Heavenly Father. Wow! That hurt! Now, realizing that I did not have a good relationship with my earthly father, I did not desire to have that type of relationship with my Heavenly Father. I realized that I had trust issues with people, and though I often said I trusted God, my Father, He showed me that I didn't trust Him either, at least not to the degree that He desired. So, this particular night, I began to cry out to God about being my daddy and, as I cried out to Him, something began to break up inside! I began to cry out to my earthly father as to why he didn't love me, why he rejected me, and why I wasn't the apple of his eye! I cried and cried that night, but during the midst of the tears, I began to feel a peace come over me. I released my earthly father that night and allowed my Heavenly Father to rescue me from the bitterness and pain I had carried since I was a little girl.

He allowed me to see that, even though the rejection of my earthly father hurt, it was a form of protection for me. My baby sister later revealed that, though she appeared to be the apple of his eye, he used to repeatedly sexually abuse her. God allowed me to see that He has been a father to me from the beginning. He gave me great godparents who took me, nurtured me, and surrounded me with love. He has placed me in some families with friends, and He has placed me in great church families that have helped me to survive.

I can look back now and understand that God has kept me closer than I wanted to be kept most times. During times of complete pain and turmoil, through periods of rejection, through stages of rebellion, through all of the ups and downs of life, He has kept me! Though the progression has been slow and tedious, I could not and did not give up. With each stage and step, I went from faith to faith and glory to glory. When I was able and ready, through God's guidance and strength, I was able to move from one level to another. I learned to love Him and praise Him more. I learned that my praise took me through, pushed me over, and brought me closer to being in His presence. I had to learn to submit my will to His will, and I had to learn that I could be my own worst enemy by trying to do things of my own free will. I had to learn that, to overcome, I had to read the Word, trust the Word, and be the Word. There were people, places, and things I had to change. There were things I had to accept about myself that needed to change, and there was the Word and Will of God that I needed to accept to become the person God intended. I had to learn forgiveness, so my Father could forgive me and learn to love others in spite of whether they appeared to love me back. It is God's will that we live an abundant life, that we forgive one another, and that we love ourselves so that we can love our neighbors. It is God's will that we overcome the enemies in our lives by leaning and depending on Him. God's promises are yea and amen! But we must know what the promises are to believe them. It is God's will that we live life to the fullest with abundance and prosperity. It is God's will that we submit our will to His will and follow His commands. God promises that, when man's ways are pleasing to Him, He will make his enemies be at peace with him. What the enemy meant for my evil was used by God for my good!

I am still a work in progress. However, learning to forgive myself, others, and walking in knowing that God continuously forgives me, I am much freer to engage in this life. God forgives me daily, even minute by minute, so who am I to hold unforgiveness towards someone else? When you understand the devastating effect of unforgiveness, and you know that the Eternal, Everlasting Father continues to forgive you of the things you do to trespass every day, you should be quick to forgive the trespasses of others.

Chapter Eight

Conclusion and Application: Putting it to Work

T he bottom line is this: the Bible states that a man born of a woman is short-lived and full of trouble (Job 14:1)! As humans, Christians or not, life has a way of interjecting pain and sorrows. The difference between Christians and non-Christians should be the way we handle the troubles we face and the expected outcome. You see, our God, who is the great I Am, Jehovah, Eternal God, Almighty, Elohim, El Shaddai, has given us promises through His inspired Word. He is not a man that He should lie, and therefore, His Word and promises can be relied on and trusted. We must be familiar with who He is and what His Word says so that we can become more than conquerors and victorious over our enemies. When we become saved, we are given a measure of faith that carries us from day to day. However, that measure is designed to grow and take us higher. The measure given is a building block, a cornerstone, that is the foundation for us to build upon and grow from faith to faith and from glory to glory.

God wants us to be healed, healthy, and whole. He wants this not only for our pleasure but so that we can work effectively in the kingdom. Hurting people hurt people and, thus, the things that cause pain in us will ultimately cause pain in others. Sometimes this is an unconscious act, and other times, it is a mean spirit that has developed in us gets pleasure out of being mean to others. I was like that until God's lovingkindness changed me. Begin the self-assessment and ask God to show you the way God sees you. Ask Him to give you the desire and strength to change the things that He reveals to you. Have patience with yourself as you begin the healing process and don't try to rush through it by jumping over the steps you need to take. As God shows you that you can trust Him, you will start trusting others as well.

Start by investigating the iniquities in your bloodline by looking at the things that have affected your family down through generations. Sometimes this can be done by doing a genogram that helps to define issues on both sides of the family. Stop focusing on your inadequacies and failures and begin to focus on who God says you are to Him. Do a gifts assessment to discover your spiritual gifts and begin to identify your passions and talents and develop them. Learn to forgive as God the Father forgives you each day. Desire to change, willingness to grow, and desire to continuously grow in God and His grace. Read His promises, learn His signs, and apply them to every situation that comes up against you. Drop the spirit of pride that can perpetuate the lie that you have it all together and don't have an issue. Seek counseling, if you must, so that they can help you navigate through the maze of questions and confusion that sometimes arise when we seek to make changes. I would suggest that you take a look at your relationships and see how they affect you and how you affect them. Trying to change in your own strength can become overwhelming and at times seem impossible. With God's power, you can become healed and whole. Reach out to God and pray through the process by asking Him to reveal the areas that need changing and be willing to make the changes.

God has healed me in so many areas, and I am still a work in progress. I made peace with my mother years before she died by looking at myself and my weaknesses and how I reacted to the struggles in our relationship instead of trying to fit her into my world. I learned, through my relationship with her, that I can't change others; I can only change myself. By the time my mother passed away, we were able to sit down and hold excellent conversations that left her in awe of the changes in us. She would often comment after these conversations by saying, "Who would've thought we could sit down and talk, mostly about the Bible, like we did." I made peace with other family members, and I made peace with myself. I made peace with the world around me by attempting to change the things I could and letting God handle the things I couldn't. I made up my mind to let God take me through the process, no matter how difficult it became.

God has done some amazing things since I let go and let Him do the things necessary to do to get me where He wanted me to be. I have stumbled, I have fallen, I have bumped my head several times; but He keeps picking me back up and pushing me forward. I keep reminding myself of Romans 8:1 that says, *"Therefore, there is now no condemnation for those who are in Christ Jesus…"* When my enemies of doubt, shame, and fear try to rise up in me, I ask God to forgive me for once again trying to take control and then step back in line with Him and the Word. I have learned to move in rhythm with God and to follow His lead. It is a continuous process and, as long as we allow God to have full reign in our lives, our enemies are defeated for He will cause us to have peace in our souls and our hope in Christ to be continually renewed. We can put our feet up and rest knowing that, as long as we stay close to God's right hand, He will make our enemies our footstool. He did it for me, and He can do it for you!

About the Author

D ebra Jewell is a Richmond, VA native. She is the very proud parent of two children, five grandchildren, one great grandson, and a niece who is also a bonus daughter. She received a Bachelor of Science Degree from Old Dominion University in Norfolk, VA, in Human Services Counseling with a minor in Psychology. Debra also holds an Associate of Arts Degree in Liberal Arts from Thomas Nelson Community College in Hampton, VA, and she received certification in Pastoral Counseling, from Word of Life Counseling Training Institute in Wichita, KS.

She is a Qualified Mental Health Professional and has worked with children, youth, and families for over twenty-five years.

Debra's areas of focus and certification include: Parent Trainer, Counselor in Training for those who are Same-Sex Attracted, and their loved ones, and HIV/AIDS Case Management.

Her experience also extends to the ministerial realm as Debra is a licensed Minister who receiving training in leadership, and obtained her license from New Beginnings Church in Matthews, NC, where she was under the leadership of Dr. Michael L. Henderson, Sr. She has held active leadership roles within her church community, serving as Associate Ministers (Gethsemane Baptist Church in Newport News, VA under Rev. Dr. Dwight S. Riddick), Altar Counselor, Intercessory Prayer Team Leader, and Sunday School Teacher for Middle School.

Debra is also a member of: The National Association of Professional Women, The American Association of Christian Counselors, and The National Association for Mental Illness. She is an advocate in healing the whole man and is a speaker, teacher, and trainer on healing body, soul and spirit and hosts a weekly video blog "Wholeness Wednesdays" through My People Community Outreach Ministries.